RILEY ASKS ABOUT AUTISM

Written by **Mandy Kennick**

Illustrated & Published by
Noble Legacy Publishing

Copyrights © 2025 Mandy Kennick
RILEY ASKS ABOUT AUTISM

All rights reserved.

Illustrations © 2025 Noble Legacy Publishing

No part of this publication may be reproduced, stored in a retrieval system, or transmitted in any form or by any means electronic, mechanical, photocopying, recording, or otherwise without the prior written permission of the publisher, except in the case of brief quotations in reviews or articles.

ISBN: 978-1-911761-15-0
First Edition: September 2025
Published by *Noble Legacy Publishing Ltd*

Acknowledgments

With love and thanks to everyone who has walked beside me on this journey family, friends,

and the wonderful teachers and professionals who dedicate their lives to supporting children with autism. And to Riley, whose light and curiosity inspire every word.

"To Riley, I hope one day you realise just how special and loved you are."

RILEY ASKS ABOUT AUTISM

Riley sat beside his mum one day,
With questions in his head at play.
He'd heard some words he didn't know,
And wondered if his mum would show him
answers to the things he'd heard,
Like *"Autism"* such a puzzling word.

"Mum," said *Riley* with a frown,

"Today at school, when I sat down,
I heard the teacher say to me that I have
something called **'ASD.'**

She said it means my brain's unique, But I
don't understand, can you speak about this
word that sounds so new?

What is *autism*? Is it true?"

His mother smiled and pulled him near,

"Oh **Riley,** love, there's nothing here
To worry about or make you sad.

Autism isn't good or bad – It's just the way your brain was made, Like how some flowers bloom in shade while others love the sunny light,

Each one is beautiful and bright."

But why do I have it?" ***Riley asked,***

"Was I not good? Was I not tasked
With being normal like the rest?
Did I not try to do my best?"

His eyes grew wide with worry deep,
As if he might just start to weep.

"Oh sweetie, no!" his mum replied,

"You've done nothing wrong," she cried.
Autism isn't something earned or
something that you haven't learned.

It's not because you weren't good,
Or didn't do the things you should.
It's just the way you came to be,
Like having green eyes, don't you see?"

"Your brain works in a special way,
It helps you think and learn and play
In patterns that are all your own,
Like seeds that in your mind are sown.

Sometimes you notice tiny things
That others miss — like butterfly wings,
Or how the light dances on the wall,
Or sounds that others can't hear at all."

Riley thought about this news,

"But sometimes I get so confused
When there are lots of sounds around, Or
when my socks don't feel quite sound.

And sometimes I just need to rock or spin
around the whole block to make my body
feel just right.

Is that part of it? Is that right?"

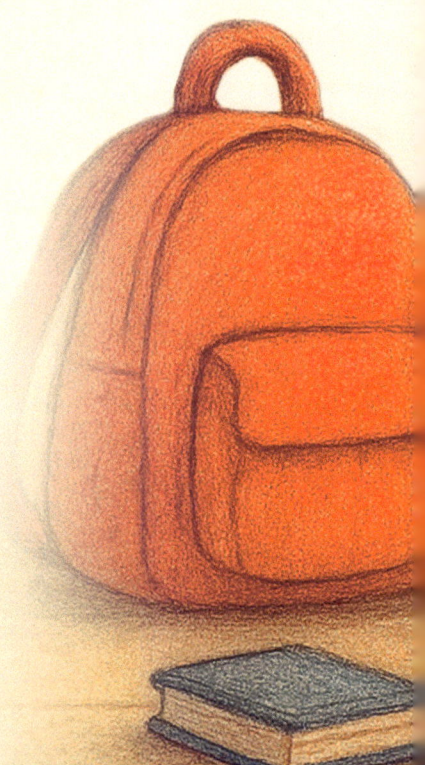

Mum Says

"Yes, darling, that's your autism too, Those feelings are a part of you.

Your senses work in their own way, They might feel stronger every day than what other children feel – But that just makes your world more real and rich with details others miss, There's beauty in a world like this."

"Some days the world feels much too loud,
With voices mixing in a crowd, And lights that seem to flash and gleam can make you want to run and scream.

But that's okay, we'll find a way
To help you through each busy day
With quiet spaces, soft and calm,
Like resting in your mother's palm."

"And when you need to move about,
To jump and spin and twist and shout,

That's your body's way to say

'I need to move to feel okay!'

So we'll make time for you to run,
To bounce and play and have some fun,

Because your body knows what's best
To help you feel calm and at rest."

Riley smiled a little smile,

"So I've been this way all the while?
Since I was born, this has been me?
It's not something I caught, you see?"

His mum nodded with a grin,

"*Yes,* love, it's been there from within.
From your very first sweet breath,
Your autism's been with you – it's not
death or sickness that will go away,
It's part of you and here to stay."

"But that means," *Riley* said with glee,

"All the things that make me, me – Like how I love to line up cars In perfect rows like little stars, And how I know each dinosaur's name and all the rules to every game, And how I notice patterns everywhere, In wallpaper and people's hair all of that is Autism too?

The special things that I can do?"

"Exactly right!" his mother cheered,

"Now I think it's become clear
That autism brings you gifts so bright,
Like seeing things in a different light.

Your memory is sharp and strong, You can remember facts so long that others would forget next day, But in your mind they always stay."

You notice when things aren't quite right,
When patterns break or colours fight.

You see the world with careful eyes
and often give us sweet surprise
with observations, smart and true,
that only someone just like you could make
with such a thoughtful mind,

So gentle, caring, and so kind."

"*But Mum,*" said Riley,

"What about the times when I just want to shout Because I can't find words to say what's in my heart throughout the day?

Sometimes my feelings get so big they make me want to dance a jig or sometimes make me want to hide with all my feelings stuck inside."

"*Oh Riley*, that's completely fine, Those big feelings are yours and mine to work through together, you and me. Sometimes feelings are hard to see or put in words that others know,

But we'll help your feelings grow into words that you can share to show others that you care."

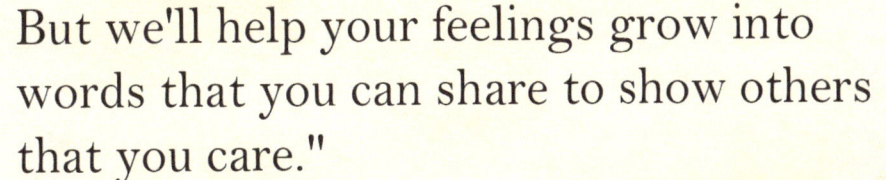

"And when you need some time alone
To think in quiet on your own,
That's not because you don't love us,
It's just your way, without a fuss,
Of sorting through the day you've had
And all the feelings, good and bad,

That filled your heart from sun to sun —
You need that time when day is done."

Riley hugged his mother tight,

"I think I'm starting to see the light.
Autism isn't something wrong,
It's been with me my whole life long.
It makes me different, that is true,
But different can be special too.
Like how no two snowflakes are the same,

"That's right, my love," his mum replied,

"And I am filled with so much pride to be the mother of a boy who brings such wonder and such joy into this world with his special way of seeing beauty every day In things that others might walk by,

You stop and look with curious eye."

"*Will other kids understand me though?*

Will they accept me as I grow?

Sometimes I worry they might think
I'm strange because I need to blink
A lot when lights are way too bright,
Or cover ears when sounds aren't right,
Or when I need to take a break From all the noise that others make."

"Some children will understand right away,
They'll want to be your friend and play.

Others might need time to learn.
That everyone deserves their turn
To be accepted as they are,

Whether they're near or whether far from
what some people call 'the norm' but you,
my love, help hearts transform."

"And if someone doesn't understand
The way you move or use your hands
To help you think or calm your mind,
We'll teach them to be more kind.

We'll help them see that different ways
Of moving through our nights and days
Are not things to fear or mock,

But treasures we should not block."

"*Your teachers know about your needs,*

They'll help you as your learning feeds
Your curious and growing mind
With knowledge of every kind.

And if you need a quiet space
Or time to slow your learning pace,
They'll understand and help you through,
Because they care so much for you."

Riley *sat in thoughtful pose*,

"I think I'm starting to suppose That having autism isn't bad, It's not something to make me sad.

It's just the way that I was made,
Like how some music's soft, some played
With trumpets loud and drums that beat –
Each song is special and complete."

"You've got it now!" his mother said,

*"Those worries we can put to bed.
You're perfect just the way you are."*

Now when **Riley** hears the word "Autism," he's no longer stirred with worry, fear, or shame inside, Instead he feels a sense of pride In who he is and how he's made, His special gifts will never fade.

He knows he's loved just as he is,

A Note for Parents and Educators

This book was written to help children understand autism in a gentle and positive way. Autism is part of how many children experience the world bringing both challenges and unique gifts.

Talking openly and kindly about differences encourages empathy, acceptance, and pride in who we are.

Resources for Further Support

- National Autistic Society (UK): www.autism.org.uk
- Autism Speaks (USA): www.autismspeaks.org
- Local support networks and educational resources in your community

About the Author

Mandy Kennick is a writer and advocate dedicated to creating stories that help children embrace themselves and celebrate differences. Inspired by her son *Riley*, she writes with warmth, honesty, and a deep belief in the power of storytelling to open hearts and minds.

Noble Legacy Publishing Ltd
www.noblelegacypublishing.co.uk

www.ingramcontent.com/pod-product-compliance
Lightning Source LLC
Chambersburg PA
CBHW041459220426
43661CB00016B/1198